D1824978

The Workin' Man's Cookbook
A Humorous Guide to Home-Cookin'

by

The Workin' Man

authorHOUSE™

1663 LIBERTY DRIVE, SUITE 200
BLOOMINGTON, INDIANA 47403
(800) 839-8640
WWW.AUTHORHOUSE.COM

© 2005 The Workin' Man. All Rights Reserved.

No part of this book may be reproduced, stored in a retrieval system, or transmitted by any means without the written permission of the author.

First published by AuthorHouse 09/09/05

ISBN: 1-4208-6543-9 (e)
ISBN: 1-4208-6542-0 (sc)

Library of Congress Control Number: 2005905361

Printed in the United States of America
Bloomington, Indiana

This book is printed on acid-free paper.

CONTENTS

WARNING

I didn't write this book to promote good health or to make you skinny like those super models you see on TV. You won't find any low fat, low cholesterol, low sodium, or otherwise crappy tastin' food here. This isn't one of those sissy Gourmet cookbooks either. Escargot ain't nothin' but snails anyway. Who do the French think they're kidding? Nouvelle Cuisine. You know what that is, brother? That's a giant plate with midget vegetables and a pine sprig on it. Proper presentation means there's got to be food present on your plate, not a bunch of weeds!

No sir, workin' men gotta eat. Real food. I use real butter from artificially inseminated, steroid fed dairy cows somewhere in Wisconsin. I cook lots of bacon and save the fat to cook my eggs in. I cook hamburgers that are about half fat, like the ones you used to get from the greasy spoon on the corner when you were growin' up. They've got ways to unclog your arteries, they haven't figured out how to make low fat taste good.

Don't worry if you don't know squat about cookin'. If you can light a burner on your stove without blowin' up the place, I can teach you the rest. I'll be behind you every step. Way behind you. Remember, cookin' ain't rocket science, it doesn't require exact measurements. You use a little of this, throw in a little of that. Experiment. Be creative. Don't be scared. Worse case scenario, you burn the house down.

The most important thing to remember is that workin' women gotta eat too. Try having a hot, home cooked meal waitin' on the table when Mama gets home from work. You just might get lucky.

Let's grab a beer and get started. I might get lucky too!

BASIC TRAINING

COOKING FOR DUMMIES

BOILING WATER

I know. It sounds simple, and it is, but there are a couple of things you have to be careful of.

Generally speaking you would boil water in a saucepan. A saucepan is the one kids used to put on their heads like helmets when they were playing army. The size of the pan, of course, depends on what you intend to cook in the boiling water. If you're boiling half a dozen eggs, I would use a medium saucepan. If you're boiling the neighbor's cat, I would use the dutch oven. A dutch oven is a really large saucepan with two small handles on it.

Once you determine the size pan you need, fill it with enough water to cover whatever you're going to boil. Don't fill it clear to the top or it will boil over. Place the pan on one of the burners on *Hi* and wait for it to come to a boil. You'll know the water is boiling when it starts to bubble, like an Alka-Seltzer.

Adding salt to the water will make food cook faster. Of course, it will give whatever you're cooking a salty flavor, if it matters. Putting a lid on the pan will also make the water boil faster, but then you can't see the bubbles and how will you know when it's boiling?

They say a watched pot never boils. That doesn't mean you can grab a beer and go finish watchin' Oprah. If you do, when you come back for another beer your water will be gone and your saucepan will be smokin' because you burnt the Teflon coating off the bottom of the pan. That will piss your wife off, trust me.

Once the water is boiling you're gonna have to put the food in it so it will cook. Be careful not to scald yourself. Cooking time varies greatly. The times shown on the boiling chart are approximate.

BOILING CHART

Hard boiled eggs — 10-15 minutes (Hint: It's best to put the eggs in cold water and bring them to a boil slowly.)

Diced potatoes —10-15 minutes

Whole chicken — 20-30 minutes (Diced chicken only 10-15.)

Spaghetti — Follow directions on the package

Minute Rice — 1 minute

Neighbor's cat — Probably a couple of hours, if you can get him to stay in the pan.

PAN FRYING

Remember that flat pan that mommy used to hit daddy over the head with when you were growing up? That's called a skillet.
That's what we use for pan frying.

Frying foods in a skillet requires some kind of cooking oil, grease, or fat. Otherwise, what you're cooking will stick to the bottom of the pan and you'll end up burning off the Teflon coating again. That'll go over real big since you already burnt up the dutch oven trying to boil the neighbor's cat. You could explain to your wife, that wouldn't happen if she would buy you some decent cookware instead of that cheap Teflon coated crap. You might get some new cookware. She'll probably smack you upside the head with the skillet. Then you'll be glad it's not a cast iron one like mom used to use!

Some meats will have enough fat of their own that you won't need to use cooking oil or grease; things like sausage, bacon, and hamburger. Stay away from turkey bacon and always use hamburger that's at least 35% fat. If you don't, you're gonna end up adding some kind of oil or grease to cook the meat with anyway. And nothin' you can buy in a can or bottle tastes as good, as good old fashioned animal fat.

For cooking chicken, pork, or vegetables you will need a generous amount of cooking oil in the bottom of the skillet. Different types of oil will give food a completely different taste. Olive oil gives food an Italian or Greek flavor. Vegetable oil has pretty much no flavor at all. I like peanut oil for stir-frying.

4

While you can buy a large variety of flavored cooking oils, I like to create my own. You can do this by adding various herbs and spices to the oil before you put the meat or vegetables in to cook. Try chopping up a couple of garlic cloves real fine, or some onion, and fry it in the oil for just a couple of minutes before you add the meat. The oil absorbs that flavor and you can taste it in whatever you're frying.

Before I fry chicken or chops I like to coat the meat in flour first. Another trick I learned is to add some spices to the flour before you dip the meat in it. Garlic salt and Italian herbs work well and I especially like *Cavender's Greek Seasoning*. Sometimes I skip the flour and just dip the meat in the spices, especially when I'm frying sirloin. Try squeezing a little lemon or lime on the meat before you dip it in the spices. I know it sounds crazy, but I find that frying steak, especially in a flavored oil, really browns the meat nicely and seals in the juices much better than broiling.

It's always best to start frying at a medium Hi temperature rather than Hi. Otherwise you end up burning the outside of the meat long before the inside is cooked. Putting a lid on the skillet will cook the inside faster and help keep the meat from drying out. Using a glass lid will enable you to view the meat while it cooks without having to take the lid off every five minutes.

Hint: To tell when chicken is done on the inside, stick a fork in it. If the chicken falls off the fork before you can lift it out of the skillet-it's done.

DEEP FRYING
Remember that dutch oven you burnt up? You're gonna need it
for deep frying.

You can buy one of those electric deep fryers, but it's just one more thing you'll have to store in your cabinets. I had a *Fry Baby*, but I got rid of it 'cause I could never find it when I wanted to use it. As the name implies, you want the oil to be deep for this kind of frying. Food should float in it. I normally use vegetable oil for deep frying most meats and vegetables, peanut oil for tempura.

Deep frying is used mostly for things like french fries, corn dogs, donuts, and hushpuppies. I call it carnival cooking. There are a few upscale dishes you can prepare in a deep fryer. Things like sweet and sour shrimp or pork, fish and chips, and tempura. Most meats will need to be dipped in some sort of batter before you fry them. The batter for corn dogs, or sweet and sour, is very heavy, almost like a cake donut. The batter for fish is much lighter. And tempura batter is very, very light.

You can find a wide variety of batters, and an occasional shortstop, in your supermarket. Usually in the meat department. Most of these batters only require that you add water. Once you have mixed the batter to the right consistency, you simply dip the meats into it and then *place* them into the hot oil. Be careful not to drop the meat into the pan, hot oil is not something you wear. Again, don't start with the oil too hot. You want to fry foods to a nice golden brown, not black.

DANGER

Listen up, or your face could end up looking like a pepperoni pizza.

Be very careful, whether you're deep frying or pan frying. Hot oil and grease likes to spatter everywhere, especially when you add water. That is why they told you in home economics never to throw water on a burning pan. It will explode! This is no shit. I always advise keeping a fire extinguisher in the kitchen, close to the stove. Be especially careful when you take the lid off a frying pan. Water condenses on the underside of the lid. When you lift it up to take a look in the pan, a few drops of that water always fall into the hot oil.

Another thing you don't want to do, is leave a frying pan unattended. I did that once. The grease caught on fire. Which in turn, caught the curtains on fire. My wife and I were sitting in the backyard sippin' a couple of pina coladas when the kid looked up and said, " Hey, Dad, I think our house is on fire! "

If you think your wife was mad when you burnt up the dutch oven and the skillet, just wait 'til you burn up her kitchen curtains!

BAKING VS. BROILING
In the center ring...

When you set your oven to *Bake* you will notice that only the bottom burner or heating coil comes on. You are cooking with the fire down below. You have probably seen your wife use the oven to bake things like cookies, pies, and cakes. You can also use the oven to bake things like casseroles and meat dishes. Baking meats usually takes longer than frying or broiling them. The advantage is that meats come out juicier because they cook in their own broth. Putting a lid on the baking dish will also make meats more tender. You may need to take the lid off for the last few minutes so that the meat can brown.

When you set your oven to *Broil,* only the top burner or coil comes on. Broiling puts the meat in direct contact with the heat source. That causes meat to brown very quickly, keep an eye on it so it doesn't burn. Sometimes when I bake meats or casseroles I like to brown them under the broiler for the last few minutes. Make sure to drain the grease from the baking dish before you do that or you could start a fire in the oven.

Broiling is kind of like using your barbecue, only inside the house. When the meat is almost ready you can brush on a little barbecue sauce and let that brown to give meats that outdoor flavor. Try brushing on some liquid smoke, Worcestershire sauce, or teriyaki while you're broiling. It helps keep the meat from drying out.

FUN THINGS TO DO IN THE KITCHEN

SAUTÉ: This is just a fancy word for frying things at a low temperature. I usually use butter or olive oil to sauté chopped vegetables, things like onions, garlic cloves, and mushrooms. All you are doing is cooking the veggies enough to make them tender, you don't even have to brown them. Try spooning some sautéed mushrooms or onions over your next steak.

STEAMING: This is a great way to get wrinkles out of your clothes. Oops, wrong book. That's in, *The Workin' Man's Travel Guide.* Don't tell anybody I said so, but steamed vegetables are much more nutritious than boiled ones. Boiling cooks away all the vitamins and minerals. You can buy one of those electric steamers, but why bother? For a couple of bucks you can get a stainless steel steam tray and use one of the saucepans that you already have at home.

TOASTING: Something you do before you belt down a glass of cheap champagne. Oops, that's, *The Workin' Man's Rules of Etiquette.* Toasting is what you do to bagels and bread, either in a real toaster or in your toaster oven. It makes them hot and crispy. You can also toast nuts by placing them on a cookie sheet and baking them in the oven. Try pouring melted butter over slivered almonds, sprinkle with sugar and cinnamon, and bake until brown.

REALLY FUN THINGS TO DO IN THE KITCHEN...

FLAMBE: This is my personal favorite. You actually pour booze over food and light it on fire. It's great for pyromaniacs. And what booze you have left over, you can drink. This is a great way to impress your girlfriend or boss, your wife knows better than to let you play with matches. Just be careful not to set your beard on fire.

BASTING: Not quite as much fun as flambe. To baste something simply means to pour liquids over it periodically. You can baste with booze, but in this case you don't set it on fire. Aw, shucks. Quite often you baste meats with their own juices, like when you baste a turkey on Thanksgiving. You can use a spoon to dip the juices over the meat or you can buy a baster at the supermarket. A baster is a plastic tube with a rubber ball on the end of it. It looks like one of those things you use to check your anti-freeze with.

SPANK MAMA WITH THE SPATULA: Shit, that's, *The Workin' Man's Sex Manual*. Never mind.

BREAKFAST

I know people are trying to eat more healthy these days,
but the thought of chokin' down a bran muffin or bowl
of oatmeal in the morning...

RED SKY AT DAWN
Wheaties aren't for everyone. Let's face it,
we're not all champions.

I don't know about you, but I hate getting up in the morning. What I want for breakfast is something to take the edge off. This tangy breakfast drink is great for hang-overs.

> 1 can of ice cold beer- a tallboy is better
> 3 fingers of *Clamoto Bloody Ceasar Cocktail Mix*
> A tall mug or glass to pour it in- chilled

Set the mug on the kitchen counter, hold three fingers up next to it. Pour in the *Bloody Caesar* mix until it comes to the top of your fingers. Add the cold beer. Enjoy.

You might say, "Hey, I gotta go to work today. I can't be drinkin' a beer for breakfast."

Think about this. You go to work and you really screw somethin' up, I mean big time. Your boss comes over to chew you out. If he smells beer on your breath he's gonna think, "Shit, Joe's been drinkin' again." He'll figure you had a bad night and that you probably won't let it happen again. On the other hand, if he doesn't smell beer on your breath, he's gonna think, "Damn, Joe's an idiot." You'll probably get fired.

If you're drunk, you can always sober up. If you're an idiot...

TEXAS ONE EYES

That's what my dumb-ass neighbor from Oklahoma calls 'em.
We call them *Moonstruck Eggs*. That's the way Cher's dad
made them in the movie.

eggs
bread
butter
beer and *Bloody Caesar*- optional

First take two slices of bread and cut a hole in the center of each slice, about the size of a tennis ball. Melt enough butter to cover the bottom of the skillet. When the butter has melted, lay the bread in the skillet. Break the eggs and pour them into the holes in the bread. Cook at a medium temperature until the eggs just turn white, turn and cook until lightly brown on the other side. I like them with the eggs cooked *over easy,* but you can cook them longer until the yolk is cooked hard.

I don't serve these with anything but a *Red Sky at Dawn*.

BAGELS AND CREAM CHEESE
I like bagels. But, Lox? What the hell is that,
some kind of Jewish Sushi?

An *Everything, Garlic, or Onion* bagel- at least 1 per person
Cream cheese- 3-4 ounces per bagel
The reddest, ripest tomato you can find
1 large red onion

This is the only way to eat a bagel as far as I'm concerned. Slice the bagel in half, horizontally so it looks like two donuts. Place the halves in the toaster or inside up in the toaster oven. Toast until brown. While the bagel is toasting, cut the red onion into very thin slices. Slice the tomato into thick slices. When the bagel is done, spread the cream cheese on the bottom half of it, real thick. Add the tomato and onion, put the lid on, and eat it like a sandwich.

My wife sometimes likes something sweet for breakfast, other than me.

An *Egg or Plain* bagel
cream cheese
Small jar of strawberry preserves or orange marmalade

Split and toast the bagel as above. Instead of adding the onion and tomato, spread the jelly, real thick, on top of the cream cheese. Do this to both halves and eat it open-faced, rather than like a sandwich. Serve with, "*Constant Comment* ", hot tea.

14

Bagel World has all kinds of flavored cream cheeses, a new flavor every week. The problem is that these flavored cream cheeses are expensive at the deli. You can make them much cheaper at home. Almost anything can be added to cream cheese; chopped green onions or olives, fresh fruits, jelly and preserves, even garlic salt and other spices. Experiment. Be **bold**. Create a whole new flavor all your own.

If bagels are a little tough for you, try putting these toppings on an English muffin or just plain toast.

THIS IS YOUR BRAIN ON FRIED EGGS

Sitting in a *Waffle House* listening to the waitresses call out orders for eggs can be very confusing. *One hard! Two over easy! Sunny side up! Scrambled!* I got high one time, back in the sixties, and just sat there all night, watching those waitresses serve breakfast. I think I've got it all figured out... if I could just remember...

SCRAMBLED

This is by far the easiest way to fry an egg. Screw this up
and your family will think *you're* on dope.

2-3 eggs- per person
1 tablespoon milk- per 2 eggs
1 stick of butter- or margarine, if you insist
diced: Velveeta cheese, ham, onions, green peppers, tomato, etc.-
optional

Break the eggs, one at a time, into a mixing bowl. (Throw the shells away, unless you're into really painful bowel movements.) Add the appropriate amount of milk. (More milk makes the eggs fluffier, but don't go overboard.) Stir the milk and eggs together with a fork.

While you are scrambling the eggs you can be melting the butter in the skillet. Once all the butter is melted, pour the eggs into the skillet and continue stirring until done. The secret to great scrambled eggs is to cook them slowly and keep stirring them. The eggs are done when they are no longer runny. They don't have to be browned, unless you like them that way.

The good thing about scrambled eggs is that you can add about anything to them; diced ham, onions, peppers, tomato, or cheese. This tastes like an omelet only it's much easier to make. My family's favorite we call *cheese eggs*. Simply cut up some *Velveeta* cheese into chunks and stir it in with the eggs. It's fabulous served with a can of corned beef hash and a slice of buttered toast.

THE HARD WAY
Sometimes bad is good and hard is easy...

1 to 2 eggs- per person
Crisco or liquid cooking oil

These are really kind of hard to screw up too. Heat the oil in the skillet, then crack the eggs, one at a time, right into the skillet. You want the yolk to break or you'll have to poke it with a fork. Fry until the egg is completely white, then turn with spatula and fry the other side for a couple of more minutes. Stick a fork in the yolk, if it is no longer runny- it's done.

The only reason I can see for cooking an egg this way is to make a sandwich out of it. An *over easy* egg is pretty nasty in a sandwich. I like an egg sandwich on toast, with lettuce, tomato, and mayonnaise, just like a BLT. I guess an egg sandwich with bacon would be called a BELT.

I like my eggs like I like my women...

OVER EASY

I don't know why they call it *over easy*, trying to flip an egg over without breaking the yolk is anything but easy. Once the oil is heated you have to break each egg very gently into the skillet, being careful not to break the yolk. Cook the egg only for a minute or two, it should still be clear and runny on top. The real trick is to try and slide your spatula under the egg without breaking the yolk. A metal spatula works best. This just takes practice, don't be upset if you crack a couple of yolks along the way. Once you have the egg on the spatula you want to just roll it over, very gently. It only needs to cook for another minute or so. Now all you have to do is get it out of the pan with out breaking it. If you've done it right, the yolk will still be runny when you cut into the egg.

Don't forget a couple of pieces of toast to sop up the yolk with.

BACON BASTED
If these don't clog your arteries, nothin' will.

1 pound real bacon- none of that turkey shit
2-3 eggs- per person
2 slices toast- per person
maybe a couple of slices of ripe tomato

This is my all time favorite way to fry an egg. First, fry the whole pound of bacon in your skillet. When the bacon is done, remove it from the pan and put it on some paper towels on a cookie sheet. Place the cookie sheet in the oven on the *lowest* setting, you don't want to catch the paper towels on fire.

Leave all of the bacon grease in the skillet. While the grease is still hot, break a couple of eggs into it, carefully, just as you would for *over easy* eggs. The beauty of basting eggs is that you don't have to turn them over. Simply take your spatula or a large spoon and start *spooning* the hot grease over the eggs. The eggs will turn white and the yolk will actually start to bubble up, it's okay. When the yolk just turns white, the eggs are ready. Don't forget that you have bacon in the oven.

I serve basted eggs on top of toast and sprinkle some bacon bits on top of that. A nice slice of tomato is the only other thing I need. Goes great with hash browns, if you're real hungry.

EGGS BENEDICK

I'll bet your in-laws from Kansas never even heard
of these damn things.

2 eggs- per person
1 English muffin- per person
2 slices of Canadian bacon or ham- per person
1 package of *Knorr Swiss* Hollandaise mix- you will need milk,
butter, and lemon for the mix. (check package for amount)
This is enough for 3-6 people.

Follow the directions on the package to prepare the Hollandaise mix. It only takes 3 or 4 minutes but, you can keep it warm while you get the rest of the ingredients ready.

Split the muffins and toast them until brown. I cook the eggs in a custard dish in the microwave. Grease the custard dishes with butter or *PAM* spray, break one egg into each bowl. Cover bowls with a paper towel and cook at 50 or 60% temperature setting. Cook for approximately 1-2 minutes, depending on how well done you want the eggs. You can heat the ham at the same time in the microwave or in the oven. When eggs are ready, place one slice of ham on each half of the English muffin, add one egg per muffin, and top with the Hollandaise sauce. Serve open-faced with sliced tomato or fruit.

OMELETS

If you really want an omelet, I suggest you go to the
Waffle House. If you're hell bent on trying, you'll need
a small skillet, preferrably non-stick.

2-3 eggs- per person
1 tablespoon milk- per 2 eggs
1 stick of butter- or margarine, if you insist
diced: Velveeta cheese, ham, onions, green peppers, tomato, etc.-
optional

Break the eggs, one at a time, into a mixing bowl. (Don't forget to throw away the shells.) Add the appropriate amount of milk. Stir the milk and eggs together with a fork.

While you are mixing the eggs you can be melting the butter in the skillet. Once all the butter is melted, pour the eggs into the skillet and cook over a medium heat. Let the eggs cook for a couple of minutes before adding the other ingredients.

When the eggs are almost done, you can tell because they won't appear to be "runny" anymore, slip your spatula under one side and flip it over. The finished product should look like an egg taco, if you're lucky.

I usually don't bother with making omelets, I just throw the extra ingredients into my scrambled eggs. It all ends up in the bottom of the crapper at the end of the day anyway.

EGGS ALA ORANGE

This is a trick I learned in Boy Scouts. The only other thing
I learned in Scouts was that some turds float.

eggs
oranges
1 campfire

If you're ever out roughing it, you know, camping in the woods, this is something you can pass on to your kids. Cut the oranges in half and eat the orange, leaving only the peel. The orange peel should be in one piece, like a little cup. Break the eggs and pour one egg into each peel. Take a pair of pliers or tongs and set the oranges right on top of the hot coals in the fire. The egg actually keeps the peel from burning while it cooks. Cook until the eggs turn white, remove from the fire with tongs and serve.

When I was a kid I always thought that turds sank, I mean they always ended up at the bottom of the toilet bowl, right? One summer, at Scout Camp, we were all out in our canoes, circled up like a bunch of covered wagons. I had to take a dump, really bad. There was no way my buddy and I could paddle back to shore in time for me to make it to the latrine. Being the resourceful scout that I was, I figured I would just hang over the side of the canoe and do my business. One more turd on the bottom of the lake wasn't going to hurt anything. So I jumped into the water, hung onto the canoe, pulled my pants down, and pinched off the finest loaf you'd ever want to see. I'm cool, I pull my pants up, and start to climb back into the canoe. All of a sudden this big turd pops up right next to me. I'm like, "Awww, shark!!!" It looked like the Spanish Armada, all those canoes paddling back to shore!

BROWN HASH..UHH...HASH BROWNS

The best ones are probably the frozen ones you buy at the supermarket. I only make my own because I like to leave the potato peels on the potato.

1 potato, 2 potato, 3 potato, 4? 5 potato, 6 potato, 7 potato, more?
1 stick of butter- at least
1 stainless steel, four sided cheese grater
1 small yellow onion- optional

While you are melting the butter in the skillet, you can be grating the potatoes. Use the side of the grater with the biggest holes in it, be very careful or you'll end up with part of your knuckles in your hash browns. Remember peelin' all those potatoes when you had KP duty? I leave the peels on, they taste better and that's the best part of the potato. Try chopping up a small yellow onion and adding it to the potatoes.

Put the potatoes in the skillet and mash them with your spatula. Pour some melted butter over them. Cook on a *medium hi* temperature until they are nice and brown on the bottom. Flip them over, mash them again with the spatula, and cook the other side until brown.

You can serve these babies with about anything.

CORNY BEEF HASH

Mom always tried to make us think she was fixing something special for breakfast. We all knew it was leftovers from the roast the day before.

Whenever I bake a roast I always make sure that I have enough beef and potatoes leftover to make hash. The next morning I chop up the beef, dice the potatoes, and toss it into the skillet with some melted butter. Stir until brown. If you don't like butter, and I don't know what planet you're from, you can just use a little water instead to warm up the hash. Serve hot.

When I cook corned beef and cabbage, I add a few potatoes and save them to make corned beef hash. Prepare the same as above.

If you don't have leftovers, the stuff in the can is fine.

PANCAKES AND WAFFLES
I would have to suggest the *Pancake House.* Their pancakes
are great and they have about a zillion flavors of syrup.

1 box of *Bisquick*
some cooking oil
a waffle iron for waffles
more patience than I have

Pancakes are just really hard to get right at home. I guess the trick is to get the griddle at the right temperature. Lightly oil the griddle and heat on *medium or medium hi.* Take a very small drop of water and drop it onto the griddle, if the griddle is hot enough the drop of water should *dance.* Pour the pancake mix slowly onto the griddle and let it spread out to the size you want your pancakes. As the pancakes are cooking they will start to bubble. When all the bubbles have popped and the batter is no longer bubbling, it is time to turn the pancakes. Once you have flipped the pancakes, the second side should take about the same amount of time as the first. Lift the pancakes occasionally with your spatula and look at the bottom until it is brown.

You make waffles the same as pancakes except you use a waffle iron to cook them with. No, you can't use this to iron your clothes with, unless they're made of gingham. If your waffle iron has a variable temperature control you'll have to play with it a few times until you get it set at the right temperature. Once you have it set- leave it there!

FRENCH TOAST

Next to the Statue of Liberty, I think this is one of the best things the French ever gave us. I do like the way they kiss...

bread- thick sliced works best, Texas toast if you can get it
eggs
milk
butter
powdered sugar, syrup, or sugar and cinnamon

Break a couple of eggs into a large flat bowl. Stir in just a little milk and scramble with a fork. Melt the butter in the skillet. When butter is melted, dip 2 slices of bread into the eggs, covering both sides. Place the bread into the skillet and fry, both sides, to a nice golden brown, turning once. Sprinkle with powdered sugar or sugar and cinnamon, or serve like pancakes with butter and syrup. I even like French toast with orange marmalade or strawberry preserves.

My wife likes it served with fresh fruit and hot tea.

SHIT ON A SHINGLE

This was my favorite meal in the army, even Sarge
couldn't screw that up.

white bread
canned or frozen creamed, chipped beef

Toast bread. Heat beef according to directions. Pour hot mixture over toast. Serve with coffee that's been in the pot for at least two days. Be glad you're too old to go back in the army.

SO MUCH FOR THE MOST IMPORTANT
MEAL OF THE DAY

LET'S DO LUNCH!

Have your machine call my machine....

SOUPS OF THE DAY

I said, "*Pea* soup, you idiot! Have you been drinkin' again?"

VEGETABLE ZOOP
Don't worry, it's got meat in it.

everything but the kitchen sink

Vegetable soup is best made with leftover roast beef, but it can be made with hamburger. If you're using hamburger you'll have to brown it first in the skillet. Chop potatoes, onion, carrots, and celery into large pieces. Boil these veggies in water for just a few minutes to soften them up. Leave the vegetables in the water, this is your soup stock. Put the leftover beef or hamburger into the pan with the vegetables. Stir in a package of *Lipton Onion Soup*. Add a couple of 14 oz. cans of stewed tomatoes. For thicker broth, also add a can of tomato sauce. Now you can get creative. Add additional cans of whatever you like; corn, green beans. lima beans, kidney beans, green peas....I don't care. Add a can of dog food- it's your soup.

Throw some macaroni in there and tell 'em it's pasta fagoli. You don't know any Italians do you?

1 POTATO, 2 POTATO, 3 POTATO, SOUP
5 potato, 6 potato, 7 potato, Poop!
This is the way mom used to make it and all five
of us kids lived. If you call that livin'.

Potatoes- duh.
1 small or medium yellow onion
a few sticks of celery
milk
butter

Boil water in medium or large saucepan. In the meantime, cut potatoes into bite size pieces. Chop up onion and celery. Put potatoes into pan and boil for 10-15 minutes, or to desired tenderness. Add onion and celery for about the last five minutes of boiling.

Pour water off of potatoes. You can use a colander. I was just waiting to see if you dumped the potatoes down the disposer with the water. A colander has nothing to do with your colon. It's a pan or bowl with holes in it for draining things. (Not your lizard!)

Once you have properly drained the potatoes put them back into the saucepan. Add about a half a stick of butter and pour in enough milk to cover the potatoes. Heat on a low temperature, constantly stirring. Serve with oyster crackers. For a change, try using popcorn instead of crackers.

Add a can of cream corn to this and you've got corn chowder.

POTATO MARY
Some free medical advice...

I suppose this is as good a place as any to tell this story. Did you know that a boiled potato can be used as a poultice? A poultice is a soft, warm mass applied to an inflamed body part. My mom told me that, she was a nurse, before she started spittin' out all of us kids.

I had a boil a few years back, and it was killin' me. So I called Ma. She told me to cut up a potato, boil it, and place a piece of it on the boil. The potato was supposed to draw the poisons out of the boil and bring it to a head. I could then stick the boil with a straight pin and squeeze the pus out, thus relieving the pressure and the intense pain. Sounded good to me, I was ready to try anything. I only made one mistake, I neglected to tell Mom where this boil was located on my body.

Imagine my wife's surprise when she walked in the front door and found me laying there on the living room floor with my legs spread-eagled in the air. I had a mirror in one hand, trying to look at my butt; and a piece of hot potato in the other, trying to shove it up my anus! My wife laughed so hard, she cried. I was in tears too, but only because I had given myself second degree burns.

The poultice didn't work and I ended up at the doctor the next day. Turns out it wasn't a boil after all. It was a #$@& hemorrhoid. To this day the guys at work call me, *Heir Kartoffel Kaupf.* I think it means *Mr. Potato Head* in German.

BEER CHILI
This is what I eat before a fartin' contest.
I haven't lost one yet.

1 lb. ground beef- (hamburger)
1 can stewed or whole tomatoes- 14 oz.
1 package chili mix
1 can of beer

You can find the chili mixes in with the spices. Most mixes call for just hamburger, stewed tomatoes, and maybe water. Fix according to the directions on the package.   Add in about half the can of beer. Drink the rest.

I like to chop up some onion and grate some cheddar or *Velveeta* cheese to add to the chili as I serve it. I also add a little vinegar or ketchup. Try serving it with tortilla chips or *Frito's,* instead of crackers.

I wouldn't recommend this before a first date, especially you gay guys. You'll be whistlin' more than *Dixie.*

UNCLE HOOSIES CONFOUNDED,
CURE FOR THE COMMON COLD

This soup will kick your ass. It's great if you're coming
down with a cold or sore throat.

chicken bouillon
crushed red pepper
garlic salt
cayenne pepper
sliced jalapeno pepper
onion
fresh garlic clove
datil or tabasco pepper

Chop the onion, fresh garlic, and peppers into very fine pieces.
Start a cup of water boiling in a small saucepan. Stir in a very
generous amount of the chicken bouillon, the broth should taste very
salty. Add in all other ingredients. After water comes to a boil,
lower heat and simmer for a couple of minutes to let the spices cook
into the broth. Drink this from a cup and finish any spices that are
left at the bottom.

This stuff works like voodoo on the flu bug.

SALADS

I know, lettuce is rabbit food. If you add in enough bacon bits
and boiled eggs you can make anything taste good.

HONEYMOON SALAD

Lettuce alone.

POPEYE'S SALAD
Did you ever have sexual fantasies about Olive Oil?

        Bag of fresh leaf spinach
        pound of bacon
        half a dozen eggs
        few small fresh mushrooms
        couple bunches of green onions
        some crumbled Blue Cheese
        apple cider vinegar
        sugar
        small bag of walnuts

You won't need the whole pound of bacon for the salad, but you will need all the grease for the dressing. You won't need all six eggs either, unless you're making a hell of a big salad. I just like to keep a couple of boiled eggs in the fridge for a snack later. Get the bacon started frying in the skillet. You can have the eggs boiled ahead of time, or start them now, with the bacon.

While the bacon is frying, wash the spinach, shake it or pat dry with a paper towel. Tear into large pieces in a serving bowl. Slice mushrooms, chop onions into 1/2 inch pieces, add these and crumbled cheese to the spinach. Remove eggs from pan and let stand in cold water for a couple of minutes. Remove bacon from skillet and set aside on paper towels. Add walnuts to bacon grease and fry until brown. Reduce heat under skillet, give the grease a chance to cool a little before you add the vinegar. Add 1/2 cup of vinegar and stir in 1/2 cup sugar. Let this simmer, stirring occasionally. Peel the eggs and cut into quarters. Break bacon into bits. Add egg and bacon to salad. When the dressing is nice and hot, pour it over the salad and mix greens with salad utensils to cover evenly.

BARAZ SALAD

I got this from the sweetest little Iranian woman you'd ever want to meet. She didn't speak a word of English though, and it took forever to figure out what the hell she was talkin' about. I think my translation is roughly correct, except she kept yelling something about *the ship of the desert!* I think she was talking about a camel. I left that part out, man.

1 head each iceberg and Romaine lettuce
3 medium potatoes
4-5 hard boiled eggs
red, green, and yellow peppers
1 ripe tomato
1 medium red onion
1 can of small black olives- pitted
8 ozs. crumbled Feta cheese
half a dozen *Greek Salad Peppers*

Boil the potatoes and eggs in one saucepan, let cool. Chop into bite size pieces: peppers, onion, tomato, potato, and boiled eggs. Wash and drain lettuce, tear into pieces and put in large salad bowl. Add all other ingredients.

For the dressing use one part olive oil to 2 parts each, vinegar and lemon juice. Sprinkle generously with *Jane's Krazy Mixed Up Salt.* Pour over salad.

This is a meal in itself. Serve with toasted pita bread.

PEANUT POTATO SALAD

I served this at a family reunion once, nobody could get past
the fact that I had left the peels on the potatoes.
You can take a hillbilly out of the hills, but...

half a dozen potatoes
medium yellow onion
about a cup of hamburger dill pickles
3-4 hard boiled eggs
1-2 cups salted peanuts
yellow mustard
mayonnaise

Cut potatoes into bite size pieces or slices, boil until tender. You
can boil the eggs in the same water. Chop up onion and pickle slices.
Let potatoes and eggs cool. Peel eggs and chop into chunks. Put all
ingredients into a mixing bowl. Stir in enough mayonnaise to cover
and add just a little mustard to taste. If you're going to let this set
in the fridge for awhile before you serve it, I would wait to add the
peanuts. You want them to be crunchy when you serve the salad.

GARLIC SLAW

I had a friend who ran a nice little restaurant and bar
in my home town. People came from all over to eat his slaw.
It was a secret recipe and he made me swear on my mother's
grave that I would never give it to anyone. He went
out of business and Ma's still kickin', so....

1 head iceberg lettuce
1 small yellow onion
2-3 cloves fresh garlic
garlic salt
about a cup of mayonnaise

The secret is using lettuce instead of cabbage to make the slaw.
Chop up the lettuce, onion, and garlic cloves real fine, and put it into
a mixing bowl. Sprinkle generously with garlic salt, depending on how
strong a flavor you want the slaw to have. Put in the refrigerator
and let stand for about an hour. The garlic salt will pull the water
out of the lettuce, leaving it kind of wilted. Leave this juice in the
bowl, it becomes part of the dressing. When you're ready to serve
the slaw simply stir in the mayonnaise and enjoy.

NUTTY BANANA SALAD
The fun part is asking your wife to come home for lunch
and peel your banana.

1 banana- per person
1 jar chunky peanut butter
1 jar mayonnaise or *Miracle Whip*
1 head of lettuce

Lay one whole leaf of lettuce on a small plate for each salad. After your wife peels your banana, have her split it, lengthwise, right down the middle. Lay the banana halves on the leaves of lettuce. In a small mixing bowl stir together equal parts peanut butter and mayonnaise. Mom used *Miracle Whip* when we were kids, it has a little sweeter flavor. Spread this on top of the bananas and serve cold.

This would actually be pretty good served with a chicken salad sandwich.

PAINLESS PASTA SALAD

We like to take this to the beach with us. Pack it into some plastic sandwich bags and throw it in your cooler. Take along some plastic silverware and you've got a nice little lunch.

1 bag of your favorite pasta- we like the curly kind
    that comes in different colors
diced ham- or pepperoni
diced onions, green peppers, and tomatoes
diced cheddar cheese
1 bag of frozen green peas
Italian salad dressing- not the creamy kind

Cook pasta according to directions, drain, and let cool. Add all other ingredients. If you let this sit in the refrigerator for a few hours or overnight, the pasta picks up some of the flavor of the other ingredients, especially the dressing.

This is a great dish for traveling when you get tired of sandwiches.

NUKE THE CUKES

To this day this salad reminds me of Summer when I was growin' up. We always had a garden, pulled the onions right out of the ground and the cucumbers off the vine ourselves.

2-3 large cucumbers
2-3 medium yellow onions
apple cider vinegar

Slice cucumbers and onions into 1/4 inch slices, place in a *Tupperware* mixing bowl. Salt and pepper lightly and cover with a mixture of 2 parts vinegar to 1 part water. Put the lid on the mixing bowl and let stand, or sit, in the fridge overnight.

If you like things a little spicy you can sprinkle in a little crushed red pepper.

SANDWICHES

My favorite is me between a blonde and a red head. Then my wife gave me a knuckle sandwich and I woke up.

HOW TO GRILL A CHEESE SANDWICH
Take it down to the Precinct and put it under a bright light,
"Where were you on the night of..."

bread
cheese
butter

I like to use at least two kinds of cheese on a grilled cheese sandwich, *Velveeta* and mild cheddar. Try adding some white cheese, like Jack or Provolone. Slice the cheese and place it between two pieces of bread. Butter one side of the bread and put it, butter side down, in the skillet. Butter the top slice. Cook at a medium temperature until nicely browned, turn it over, press with your spatula, and cook the other side until brown. The cheese should be melted. When the sandwich is ready you can open it up and add a slice of tomato or hamburger dill pickles. Try dipping your grilled cheese in ketchup.

To make it a grilled ham and cheese, simply put some sliced ham on top of the cheese before you grill it.

SOMETIMES YOU GET CHICKEN SALAD
Sometimes you get chicken...

    4 large crescent rolls
    2 cans white chicken- 5 oz. size
    5 oz. can of chunky pineapple
    a handful of salted cashews
    1 small yellow onion
    1 stick of celery
    about a cup of mayonnaise

Cut onion and celery into small pieces. Put chicken into a small mixing bowl. Add other ingredients and stir in mayonnaise. This can be placed on a leaf of lettuce and served as a salad. I would serve that with some sliced tomato, boiled eggs, and crackers. Or, put it in the crescent rolls and eat it like a sandwich. Serve with fresh fruit.

This is kind of a girlie meal, something you'd eat with your wife on a Saturday afternoon on the porch. Not something you'd want to bring in your lunch to the packing plant.

TACO BURGERS

Some of you young bucks have probably never even heard of these. They used to serve them at every fast food Mexican joint in town, now I can't find them anywhere.

1 lb. hamburger
1 package taco seasoning
lettuce
tomato
cheddar cheese- shredded
hamburger buns

Fix the taco meat according to the directions. Place the meat on the buns, add shredded cheese first, then lettuce, then a slice of tomato. Top and serve. Use *Louisiana Hot Sauce* as a condiment instead of taco sauce. Don't forget the cold beer.

TAKHOMA BURGER

When I was growin' up the *Takhoma Burger* was the greasiest little burger joint you ever saw. It was run by a grumpy old man that everyone called, "Arkie". I think we called him that because he was from Missouri. There were no tables inside, it was strictly carry out. It was close to downtown and at lunch people would line up outside of it for blocks; doctors, lawyers, secretaries, bank tellers, construction workers, and every hippie in the tri-state area. Arkie served his burgers with mustard, pickle, and onion only. If you wanted ketchup you had to ask for it. If you wanted lettuce and tomato, forget it. Arkie would tell you where you could get a nice salad and point you in the direction of the diner on the corner.

To make one of Arkie's famous burgers you take a handful of hamburger, not too lean, and squash it together with a good pinch of finely chopped yellow onions. Mash it with your hands into the thinnest patty you can make. Sprinkle with salt and fry in a skillet until meat is crispy. Put the top of the bun on the hamburger for about a minute before you take it from the pan. Serve with mustard, pickle, and another pinch of fresh chopped onions. Great with Santa Monica Pier potato chips.

SANTA MONICA PIER POTATO CHIPS

I know this isn't a sandwich, but it goes here, next to the hamburgers. There used to be a place on the pier that served nothing but these fries in brown paper bags. I don't know if it's still there or not.

Remember that four sided cheese grater that you used to make hash browns? You'll need it to slice these fries. On one side of the grater you'll find a couple of slots for slicing rather than grating. Use this side to slice your potatoes, lengthwise, as thin as you can. The potatoes will want to stick together, so you'll have to kind of separate them as you put them into the hot oil. I recommend deep frying for the best results. You may also need to stir the fries a little so they don't stick together while they are cooking. Fry the potatoes to a nice golden brown.

While the potatoes are frying, take a couple of brown sandwich bags and shake some salt into them. When the fries are ready, remove them from the pan. Hold them over the pan for just a moment to let the oil drain off. Drop them into the paper bags and shake. Eat them right out of the bag.

Try dipping these in sour cream or your favorite potato chip dip.

CHEEKY CHIP DIP
Mom always said this was her favorite dip, next to me.
It isn't a sandwich, I know, but it's gotta go here.
Next to the chips.

    8 ozs. cream cheese
    2 tablespoons of mayonnaise
    1 tablespoon of horse radish

Put the ingredients into a small bowl and mash together with a fork. Dip your chips in it and eat.

ERIN AND JAMIE'S BT SANDWICHES

Okay, we're back to sandwiches. I got a little side tracked.
Sue me.

    white bread
    fresh sliced tomatoes
    butter

I *invented* this sandwich about 25 years ago, quite by accident. I was baby sitting for a couple of rugrats and they kept whining about having sandwiches for lunch. I couldn't find anything in their mom's house; no lunch meat, no tuna, no hot dogs, no hamburger, I couldn't even find ketchup or mustard. I offered to make them banana splits, but they insisted on sandwiches for lunch. I had to come up with something or risk going to jail for kidslaughter.

All I could find was some white bread, a couple of tomatoes, and some butter in the fridge. So, I made sandwiches out of that. I buttered both pieces of bread, put a couple of slices of tomato on it, with a little salt and pepper, and served it cold.

The kids have both grown up now and have kids of their own, but they still remember the first time I made butter and tomato sandwiches for them. To this day it remains their favorite lunch.

OPEN FACED

This is a great way to use up leftover meat and potatoes
from the night before.

leftover turkey or roast beef
bread
1 package of chicken or brown gravy mix- you can buy it in a jar

Prepare gravy according to directions. Heat up the meat and put it on a couple slices of bread on a large dinner plate. Pour the hot gravy over the meat and bread. This is normally served with potatoes and gravy. It makes a quick and easy hot lunch.

A RUBE'S REUBEN
As easy to make as a grilled cheese.

loaf of rye bread
can or jar of sauerkraut
sliced corned beef
sliced Swiss cheese
thousand island dressing

Warm the corned beef and sauerkraut first, either in the microwave or, preferably, in a skillet. Butter one slice of the bread and place it in a skillet, add, in this order, corned beef, sauerkraut, and Swiss cheese. Butter the other slice of bread and put it on top. Mash down on the sandwich with your spatula, cook until brown, turn, brown other side. When sandwich is ready, remove from pan, lift top, and add thousand island dressing.

I serve this with a Kosher dill pickle and some peanut potato salad. And a cold beer, of course.

You can call me what you want, just don't call me late for

DINNER

APPETIZERS

I know you're already hungry, so we're gonna skip this part.
A workin' man doesn't need anything but a cold beer for an
appetizer anyway.

SIDE DISHES

I like a tall brunette...

GET STEWED TOMATOES

My wife hates soggy bread, she can't even stand to watch me eat it. I reckon that's why I like it so much.

2 cans of stewed or whole tomatoes
4-5 slices of white bread
white or brown sugar

Pour tomatoes into saucepan, break whole tomatoes into smaller pieces. Tear bread into bite size pieces and add to the tomatoes. Add sugar to taste and stir until tomatoes are hot and sugar is dissolved.

Try adding a can of green beans to this, you won't need any other side dishes.

4077TH POTATOES
The skinny on mashed potatoes.

potatoes
water- for boiling
1 stick of butter
some milk
maybe a potato masher

Start the water boiling in a saucepan while you are cutting the potatoes into large chunks. Leave the peel on the potato! Boil potatoes until they fall apart when you stick them with a fork. If you like chunky mashed potatoes don't boil them for so long. Drain potatoes, return to medium heat. Add half a stick of butter. Start mashing potatoes with a masher or fork. Add in milk slowly until they reach desired consistency.

For a little variety add some cheddar cheese to the potatoes. Save the leftovers, you can make them into patties and have potato pancakes in the morning.

MICKEY RONI AND CHEESE
You can buy it in those boxes with everything already in it.
But Mom always made it from scratch and *that's the way uh huh,
uh huh, I like it. Uh huh.*

1 box of macaroni
1 stick of butter
about a cup of milk, maybe a little more
Velveeta cheese, cut into large chunks
cheddar cheese- optional

Boil macaroni according to directions, drain when tender. Put macaroni back into saucepan and heat at low temperature. Add about half that stick of butter and stir. When butter is melted pour in enough milk to cover the macaroni. Drop in pieces of *Velveeta*. The cheese will melt and turn the milk into a cheese sauce. You want to serve this before all the cheese melts so that there are some chunks of cheese left in the macaroni.

If you like baked macaroni, the kind with browned cheese on top, here's what you do. Follow the same directions as above to make macaroni and cheese in your saucepan. Spray some *Pam* into a small baking dish. Pour the macaroni and cheese from the pan into the dish. Cover with grated cheddar cheese. Place in the oven and broil at about 400 degrees until the cheese on top turns brown.

Add some chunks of ham and it becomes a main course.

STRUNG OUT BEANS AND NUDE POTATOES
It's gonna be a sad day when the flashbacks go away.

It is absolutely imperative that you use only *fresh* string beans
1 small bag of new potatoes
3-6 strips of bacon- the pork variety!

Start the water boiling in a large saucepan, put the steaming tray in. Break the stems off of the string beans, otherwise leave them whole. Put beans, potatoes, and bacon in to steam until the beans are tender. I can eat this for a meal.

GOMBO
You might not like this, if you're a damn Yankee.

fresh okra
1 or 2 cans of stewed or whole tomatoes
1 medium yellow onion
2 stalks of celery
1 green pepper
1 cup cooked white rice

Chop onion celery, and green pepper into medium chunks. Slice okra into 1/2 inch pieces. Pour tomatoes into a saucepan, add vegetables and simmer over medium heat until okra is nice and tender. This will probably take at least 20-30 minutes. You can prepare the rice ahead of time or while the stew is cooking. I would wait and pour the rice in about 10 minutes before you're ready to serve.

Feel free to throw in a little cayenne pepper or *Louisiana Hot Sauce.*

MR. GREEN BEAN'S CASSEROLE

This is the dish that all the little old ladies bring to the covered dish dinner at church on Sunday night.

2 cans of green beans
1 can of cream of mushroom soup
2 cans of those crispy onion rings

Drain beans and pour into a baking dish sprayed with *Pam*. Thin the soup with about a half a can of water and pour over the beans. The soup should just cover the beans. Cover the top with the onion rings. Go ahead, use them all. Bake at 450 degrees for 30 to 40 minutes.

Take it to church on Sunday night. Maybe you'll meet a nice little old lady.

THE SECRET TO CORN ON THE COB

Sure, anybody can boil corn on the cob. But you know what makes it great? Add a little milk to the water as you boil it.

You can also try fried corn on the cob. Or cut it into 1 inch pieces and put it on the skewers next time you make shish kabobs. You can roast corn in your campfire by leaving the husks on and putting it right on the coals.

ARTI'S CHOKED HEARTS

I never had an artichoke heart until we moved to Los Angeles.
Those fruits and nuts will eat anything.

First you have to make sure the artichokes are ripe. A ripe artichoke will be kind of purple on the bottom. To cook, simply cut the stem at the bottom and place in boiling water for about an hour. Serve with melted butter and /or a small dish of mayonnaise. Peel the leaves off and dip them in the butter or mayonnaise. Then you kind of scrape the inside of the leaf off with your teeth. Don't eat the whole leaf, just the soft part on the inside of it. When you've eaten all the leaves what's left is the artichoke heart. On top of the heart you'll see some stuff that looks like green hair, scrape it off with a spoon or fork and throw it away. Dip the heart in butter or mayo and enjoy.

This is the perfect accompaniment to seafood, especially shell fish.

THE ELECTRIC DILL

This really isn't something you eat. It's just a fun way
to show your kids how the electric chair works, you know,
if you're ever sittin' around the table talking
about the death penalty.

1 extension cord- indoor type
2-8d nails
1 or 2 large dill pickles

Find a short extension cord, the kind you use inside your house, it is made with zip cord. Cut the *female* plug off, leaving only the *male*. The *male* end is the one that plugs into the wall. (I'm sittin' here thinkin', *if I gotta explain this to you, maybe you shouldn't try this at home*. Aw, what the hell, it's only 110...go for it!) Split the zip cord and peel it back about a foot. Strip the wires back about an inch. Take the bare end of each wire and wrap it tightly around one of the nails. Don't wrap the wires around the same nail.

Now, wait 'til it gets dark. Take your pickles out on the back porch. Stick one nail into each end of the pickle. Stand back and plug it in. Watch that baby spark and sputter. It glows in the dark!

This should keep the kids entertained for hours. I don't think it'll give them any bad ideas.

THE MAIN COURSE

I won't even go there.

DON'T LET YOUR MEAT LOAF

The best thing about meat loaf is that you can make cold meat loaf sandwiches with the leftovers.

2 lbs. hamburger- for this I use leaner meat, like ground round
cup and a half of crushed up saltine crackers
2 eggs
cup and a half of ketchup
1 cup brown sugar

Place hamburger a large mixing bowl. Add raw eggs and crushed crackers. Mash all this together in your hands, your kids will love to help you. Place this in a bread pan, preferably Pyrex. Mix ketchup and brown sugar in large measuring cup or bowl. Pour sauce over hamburger and spread evenly to cover. Place in oven and bake at 400 degrees for 45 minutes to an hour.

This is the basic recipe for meat loaf, it can be prepared ahead of time and left in the refrigerator overnight.

Using this basic recipe you can create a whole variety of dishes simply by stuffing the meat loaf with your favorite cheeses or vegetables. To stuff a meat loaf you will need some wax paper. Lay a piece of wax paper on your cutting board. Wipe it with *Crisco* or spray it with *Pam* so that meat won't stick. Smash the meat loaf as flat as you can with your hands. Lay the other sheet of wax paper over the meat. Take a rolling pin and roll the meat out as thin as you can. Remove the top wax paper and cover the meat evenly with grated cheddar cheese. Use the wax paper to help you *roll* the meat loaf up like a jelly roll. Place the rolled up meat loaf into a bread pan and cook the same as above.

You can stuff a meat loaf with anything you want. Add some diced potatoes to the cheddar cheese, it's like scalloped potatoes. Make an Italian *pizza loaf,* add the same ingredients you would use to make a pizza; green peppers, onions, black olives, even pepperoni. Top with pizza sauce instead of ketchup. For Mexican meat loaf, add picante sauce, cheddar and jack cheese, onions, and jalapenos if you like it hot. Serve with sour cream.

You've got the idea. Let your imagination run wild.

ROBERT GOULASH

I got this recipe from a fat old Hungarian woman with a dark mustachio. Damn my wife's mom can cook!

1 box of macaroni
1 lb. of hamburger
1 can stewed tomatoes
1 can tomato sauce
1 medium yellow onion

Boil macaroni in a large saucepan until tender. While macaroni is cooking, brown hamburger in skillet. Add chopped onions to the hamburger for the last couple of minutes. Drain macaroni and return to saucepan. Pour in stewed tomatoes and tomato sauce, add hamburger and onions. Simmer on low heat for 10-15 minutes.

This is the basic recipe for goulash. You can add corn, green beans, peppers, celery, just about any vegetables you like.

CRACK-POT ROAST

If you don't have a crock pot, go out and get yourself one right now. Next to the microwave oven it's the best thing ever invented for the workin' man.

2-3 lb. beef or pork roast
6 potatoes
6 carrots
3 medium yellow onions
1 package of onion soup or 1 can of tomato soup

First brown your roast in the skillet, I use olive oil with some garlic salt sprinkled in it. Cut potatoes into bite size chunks, slice onions lengthwise into sixths, slice carrots into 2 inch pieces. When meat is brown put it in the bottom of the crock pot. Add vegetables on top of meat. Mix onion soup with 2 cups water and pour over meat and vegetables. Set crock pot to Hi and cook for six hours.

The great thing about a crock pot is that you can leave food in it to cook all day without burning it. Brown your roast the night before, cut up your vegetables and let them soak in a mixing bowl full of water overnight. Before you go to work the next morning, simply put the ingredients in the crock pot, cover, set to low temp, and leave it to cook while you're at work all day. Set temperature to Hi about half an hour before you're ready to serve.

You can try adding some cabbage, fresh green beans, or anything you like to your pot roast. You will not believe how tender the meat is when it's cooked in a crock pot.

CRACK-POT CORNED BEEF
This is a must on St. Pattie's Day.

1 corn beef brisket
1 head cabbage
4-6 potatoes
1 keg green Irish beer
1 leprechan

Brown the brisket in a skillet. Cut the head of lettuce in half, lengthwise. Cut those halves into thirds. Cut potatoes into bite size pieces. Add extra potatoes if you plan on using leftovers to make corned beef hash for breakfast. Put meat in bottom of crock pot, add cabbage and potatoes, pour in about 2 cups of beer.

Drink the rest of the keg and go with friends to the St. Pattie's Day Parade. The corned beef and cabbage will be just as stewed as you are when you get home.

REMEMBER THE ALAMO RICE

I learned how to make this from some Mexican family down in Brownsville, Texas. Just before immigration took them away.

2 cups cooked white rice- *Minute Rice* is as good as any
1 lb. hamburger
chopped yellow onion, celery, and green pepper
14.5 oz. can of stewed tomatoes
8 oz. can of tomato sauce
garlic salt
chili powder

Sprinkle hamburger with garlic salt and chili powder, brown in skillet. Just before meat is done add in chopped vegetables and brown slightly. Put cooked rice into large saucepan, add meat when ready. Stir in stewed tomatoes and tomato sauce and simmer over low heat for about 15 minutes. Add more garlic salt and chili powder to taste.

Serve with hot, buttered flour tortillas. Makes a great burrito stuffing.

OLIVE'S CHICKEN
Olive, what a dish....the chicken too.

1 boneless, skinless chicken breast per person
1 jar green olives- the cheap cracked ones work fine
2 small yellow onions
2-3 fresh garlic cloves
3 carrots
1 cup pine nuts or walnuts
olive oil
flour

Coat the chicken breasts in flour with a little garlic salt sprinkled in it. Slice onions and carrots. Dice the garlic cloves and brown them in olive oil in a large skillet. Place the chicken in the skillet, cover, and fry on medium hi heat for 10-15 minutes. Turn and brown other side. Test chicken with fork, when it is almost ready, add pine nuts or walnuts and fry until brown. Add olives, carrots, and onions. Cover skillet and simmer on medium heat for another 10 minutes or so.

Serve with rice pilaf. I like the *Near East* brand.

HAMBURGER PIE

The British call it *shepherd's pie*. It would be a nice hearty meal after a long day of stump-breakin' sheep.

half a dozen potatoes
1 lb. hamburger
14.5 oz. can of green beans
1 small yellow onion- chopped
15 oz. can of tomato sauce

Prepare mashed potatoes. (See 4077th Potatoes) While potatoes are boiling, brown hamburger in skillet. Drain hamburger, leave in skillet and add green beans, chopped onions, and tomato sauce. Stir and simmer for about 5 minutes. Place hamburger mix into deep baking dish. Spread mashed potatoes evenly over the top with a wooden spoon. Place in oven and bake at 450 degrees for about 20 minutes.

That is the way my wife likes it. I like to add a can of corn and stewed tomatoes. I also like it with cheese on top. If you're adding cheese, wait until about the last 10 minutes or so. This really is a meal in itself.

COCOANUT SHRIMP WITH JEZEBEL SAUCE
This is a Cocoa Beach favorite. To really enjoy it you have to sit at an outdoor table at the beach, get drunk, and sing Karaoke.

half a dozen large fresh shrimp per person
1 box of beer batter or batter for fish and chips- you'll probably find it in the meat department at the market
1 bag of shaved coconut- you'll find this with the flour and baking goods.

Unfortunately, you'll have to peel and devein the shrimp yourself, unless you can get the butcher to do it for you. (Ha, what are you, livin' in the fifties?) You do *not* want shrimp that has been already cooked. To devein the shrimp you must peel them first. Then lay the shrimp on it's back and slice it's belly right down the middle, lengthwise. You don't want to cut it clear in half, only deep enough to lay it open. That is how you *butterfly* shrimp. You'll see a tiny black vein in the middle of the shrimp. Remove the veins from the shrimp and discard them in the trash. If this is too much trouble you can leave the veins in, they really won't hurt anything. However, the vein is part of the shrimp's digestive system-it's got poop in it. Don't let your wife and kids see it or they won't eat it.

Prepare the batter in a mixing bowl. Pour the coconut onto a large cutting board. Heat vegetable or peanut oil in a large saucepan or dutch oven over medium hi heat. Dip shrimp, one at a time, first into batter, then into coconut. You can go ahead and coat all the shrimp and keep them on a plate until you're ready to fry them. When oil is hot carefully add shrimp and fry until golden brown. Shrimp can be put on paper towels on a cookie pan and kept warm in the oven until all shrimp are cooked and ready to serve.

JEZEBEL SAUCE
I guess they call it that because it's tart.

12 oz. jar apple jelly
12 oz. jar pineapple preserves
12 oz. jar peach or apricot preserves- or both
4 oz. jar sweet and sour mustard
1-2 tablespoons of horse radish

Mix all ingredients together in a small mixing bowl. Go easy on the mustard and especially the horse radish. Add a little at a time and keep tasting it until you get it as spicy as you like it. You can probably leave out the mustard and horse radish for most kids.

Sometimes I substitute orange marmalade in place of the other jelly and preserves. It's good on cocoanut shrimp, even without the mustard and horse radish.

If someone doesn't want the sweeter sauce you can make regular shrimp sauce simply by adding some horse radish to some ketchup. I also add some *Worchestershire* sauce and a good squeeze of lemon.

SPLIT TAIL

If you've ever had lobster at a restaurant it was probably
boiled and was kind of chewy, like rubber. The secret
is to *broil* the lobster.

1 lobster tail per person- if you like cracking the claws and such,
buy whole Maine lobster. Buy them already boiled unless you
want to listen to them scream when you drop them in the
boiling water. I buy just the 16 oz. lobster tails, the drawback
is they come frozen.
1 lemon per lobster- at least
1/2 stick of butter per lobster- plus 1 stick for broiling

Split the lobster tail in half by cutting it lengthwise right down the
middle of the belly. Crack the shell and place the lobster on a broiling
pan, kind of on it's sides with the exposed meat up. Squeeze lemon
over the meat. Melt 1 stick butter in measuring cup in microwave at
30% power. When butter has melted use a cooking brush, not a hair
brush, and brush butter over the lobster. Broil lobster until the top
is nice and brown. Prepare King Crab the same way. Serve with half
a lemon and a custard dish full of melted butter for dipping.

Arti's Choked Hearts or *Santa Monica Pier Potato Chips* make a
great side dish.

SPAM AND BEANS

I'm kidding. That's what you have the baby-sitter serve the kids when you're going out for dinner. You deserve real ham.

14.5 oz. can Great Northern beans
14.5 oz. can Navy beans
14.5 oz. can small Pinto beans or Black eyed peas
8 Ozs. diced ham
1 small yellow onion
1 box cornbread mix
butter and honey

Pour undrained cans of beans into a saucepan. Add chopped onions and ham. Simmer over medium heat for about 20 minutes, stirring occasionally. Serve over cornbread, or with cornbread and honey on the side.

Again, this is not really recommended before a first date.

KINKY KEILBASA

Maybe after dinner you can talk Mama into a game of,
Hide the Sausage...

smoked keilbasa- enough to go around
sauerkraut- enough to completely cover the keilbasa in a baking
   dish

Cut the keilbasa into 3" pieces, place in microwave safe baking dish. Cover and heat in microwave at 75% for 5 minutes. Cover with sauerkraut, replace lid and heat at 75% for another 5 minutes. This can be served on plates or in a bun as a sandwich.

I also like keilbasa with potatoes and apples. Cut potatoes and apples into large bite size pieces and place in baking dish. Cover and cook in microwave at 75% for 10-15 minutes, before adding the sausage. In conventional oven, cover and bake at 450 degrees for half an hour.

CHICKEN FRIED STEAK

If you're a meat and potatoes kind of guy, this is definitely for you. I can't think of a more hearty meal.

minute or *chopped* steak- these are really cheap at the store
a couple of eggs
a can of cracker meal- you'll probably find this next to the flour
1 package or can of chicken gravy

Break eggs into a shallow mixing bowl, whisk with fork. Pour cracker meal onto cutting board or plate. Dip steaks in egg, let excess run off, then dip into cracker meal until well coated. You can go ahead and batter all the steaks at once and set them aside. Pour a generous amount of cooking oil into a deep skillet, heat at medium hi temperature. Place steaks into skillet and fry to a golden brown, turning once. Steaks can be kept warm in the oven until all of them are ready. While steaks are frying, prepare gravy according to directions. Serve steaks smothered with chicken gravy.

I serve this dish with mashed potatoes, make sure you have plenty of gravy for both. It's also good with brown gravy.

CHICK 'N NOODLES
This could be as big as mud wrestling.

1 or 2 large packages of frozen egg noodles
4-6 chicken breasts or 1 whole cut up fryer

I like white meat only in chicken and noodles, so I use chicken breasts. If you like dark meat use a whole fryer. In either case you will want to peel the skin off the chicken before you boil it. Boil water in a large saucepan or dutch oven. Put chicken in boiling water and boil for about half an hour. You should be able to easily tear chicken off the bone with a fork when it is ready. Remove chicken from the water and set aside to cool. Put egg noodles in boiling chicken broth. I like to add a little chicken bouillon to the broth for flavor. Boil noodles until tender. While noodles are cooking remove chicken from the bones and cut or tear into bite size pieces. Add chicken to noodles and simmer on low heat for about 15 minutes.

I like to eat chicken noodles on bread, like an open faced sandwich. It's also good served over mashed potatoes.

BABY GOT BACK RIBS
You cook these in the crock pot, just like you would a roast.
The secret's in the sauce.

baby back ribs- enough to fill your crock pot
SAUCE:
2 cups ketchup
1/3 cup Worcestershire sauce
1/4 cup apple cider vinegar
1 teaspoon liquid smoke
1/2 cup brown sugar
1/2 teaspoon of each: garlic powder, onion salt, cayenne pepper
1/8 cup lemon juice

You will want to brown the meat first. You can do this by simply frying it in a skillet over medium heat until brown. Just use enough oil to barely cover the bottom of the skillet. I sprinkle a little garlic salt into the oil to add some flavor.

Mix all ingredients for the sauce in a medium saucepan. Add water to desired thickness, start with about half a cup. Simmer over low heat for at least an hour, stirring occasionally. Keep an eye on it, you may need to add more water. When sauce is ready put ribs into crock pot and pour in all of the sauce. Cook on high for about 6 hours.

You can also use this sauce with a roast to make BBQ pork or beef.

OUR JUST DESSERTS

We all get them in the end.

GRANDMA'S HEAVENLY DESSERT

This was a family favorite when I was growin' up. Luckily, my grandmother taught me how to make it before she died. It's not quite the same without Grandma in the kitchen.

2 cups miniature marshmallows
2 cups *Dream Whip*
1/2 cup milk
3 cups graham cracker crumbs- you can crush them yourself
1/2 stick margarine
1/4 cup white sugar
22 oz. can cherry pie filling

In a double boiler, melt marshmallows with milk, stirring constantly. Allow to cool, then stir in the *Dream Whip*. In a separate pan, melt the margarine and stir in the white sugar until dissolved. When sugar is dissolved add in graham cracker crumbs, stir until mixed.

Put half of the crumb mixture in the bottom of a buttered 8x8 glass baking dish. Add half of the marshmellow and whipped cream mix, spread evenly over crumbs. Spoon on all of the cherry pie filling. Add the other half of the cream mixture, spreading evenly. Top with the other half of the crumbs. Refrigerate at least 3-4 hours, or prefferably over night. Cut into squares and serve.

PINEAPPLE RIGHT SIDE UP CAKE
This is easy to make but you have to hum the theme
from *Hawaii Five-O.* Book 'em Dano.

2 eggs
1/2 cup sugar
2 Tablespoons flour
one #2 can of crushed pineapple
5 slices of white bread
1 stick butter

Drain pineapple and mix with eggs, sugar, and flour. Pour into a 8x8 buttered casserole dish. Cut bread into half inch cubes and brown in skillet with 1 stick butter. Pour bread on top of pineapple. Heat at 350 degrees for 30-45 minutes.

Must be served by a beautiful woman in a grass skirt doing the hula dance. Or, maybe you can get your wife to do it.

WAN HUNG LO'S NOODLE COOKIE
These *belly* good cookie.

2 cups Chow Mein noodles
1 small package chocolate chips
1 small package butterscotch chips
1 cup salted peanuts

Melt chips in a double boiler over medium heat. Once melted, remove from heat and stir in noodles and peanuts. Drop, by the spoonful, onto a sheet of greased wax paper. Chill in refrigerator to set.

Serve with Mai Tai's while singing, "I've been wolkin' on the lail load..."

APPLE CRUNCH
Not as American as Mom's Apple Pie but, you're not the mama.

3 cups diced apples- sweet or sour, your choice
2 Tablespoons flour
1 cup white sugar
3/4 cup oatmeal
3/4 cup brown sugar- how come you taste so good?
3/4 cup flour- in addition to the 2 Tablespoons above
1/4 teaspoon baking powder
1/4 teaspoon baking soda
1/3 cup melted butter or margarine

Mix apples, 2 Tablespoons flour, and white sugar and place in greased, 11x13 baking pan. Mix oatmeal, brown sugar, 3/4 cup flour, baking powder, and baking soda in bowl. Stir in melted butter. Spread this mix over the top of the apples. Bake at 350 degrees for about 45 minutes. Top should be well browned.

This is delicious served with ice or whipped cream. It can also be served with a slice of cheddar cheese, just like apple pie.

KILLER BROWNIES
Sounds like a bunch of Girl Scouts running around with knives.
These brownies really were killer in the sixties.

1 cup light *Karo* syrup

1 cup butter

10 oz. *Baker's Semi-Sweet Chocalate*

1 and 1/2 cups sugar

6 eggs

2 teaspoons vanilla extract

2 cups all-purpose flour

1 cup chopped walnuts

1 cup chocolate chips

Preheat oven to 350 degrees. Grease 9x13 baking pan with *Crisco*. Sift flour to cover pan. In a large saucepan bring syrup and butter to a boil, stirring occasionally. Remove from heat and stir in semi-sweet chocolate until melted. Add sugar. Stir in eggs, one at a time. Add vanilla extract. Stir in flour until everything is well mixed. Pour into pan. Sprinkle with chopped nuts and chocolate chips. Bake for about 35 minutes. Allow to cool before cutting.

Great served with homemade ice cream. You'd better at least have milk.

BEDTIME SNACKS

You're on your own...

HOT BUTTERED RUM
Yo Ho, Yo Ho, a pirate's life for me...

2 shots of spiced rum
1 slice of butter
1 teaspoon honey
1 squeeze of fresh lemon
dash of cinnamon or allspice

Mix all ingredients in a juice glass and heat in the microwave at 60% for about 30 seconds or until butter melts. It should be nice and hot when you serve it. Sip slowly and enjoy.

This will take you to a nice, soft landing in la-la land.

MILK TOAST

My dear old mother served this to me for breakfast, lunch, and dinner when I had my tonsils out. God bless her. It's actually quite nice at bedtime...it helps you sleep.

Toast two pieces of white or wheat bread. While the bread is toasting, warm up about a half a cup of milk in the microwave or in a small saucepan on the stove. Be careful not to let the milk come to a boil or it will curdle. Put the toast on a small plate and pour the warm milk over it. Salt and pepper to taste. You can butter the toast first or add a slice of butter to the milk for an even richer flavor.

This is a great dish to fix for grandma while her dentures are out for repairs.

Pleasant dreams.

Stick a fork in me, I'm done.

WHAT PEOPLE ARE SAYING ABOUT THE BOOK

Politically incorrect, sexist, childish, absolute rubbish!

My Agent

Why didn't you tell me that boil was on your anus?!

My Mom

(Uranus is a planet, Mom.)

How do you play, Hide the Sausage?

My Son

They really can do miracles with clogged arteries.
They've got this balloon....

My Dad

I don't think my mustache is that noticeable. Besides, I'm not
Hungarian. Who ever heard of Polish goulash?

My Mother-in-law

You know female facial hair doesn't skip a generation.

My Father-in-law

It'll be a cold day in Hell before you see me in a Hula skirt again!

My Wife

You're fired you idiot!

My Boss

ABOUT THE AUTHOR

First of all, I am not a chef. I cook for pleasure, not profit. (Unless this book takes off, of course.) I learned to cook primarily from my mother. When I was a teenager I was always hungry. Mom was usually preparing dinner when I came home from school and I would sneak in and try to grab a meatball or sausage from the skillet when she wasn't looking. She caught me a few times and said if I was gonna be in the kitchen, I might as well help her get supper ready. Hey, it got me out of doin' the dishes.

When I went off to college, or I should say, when I went off to a town that had a college, I got a job in a restaurant as a dishwasher. Being the industrious young lad that I was, I soon worked my way up to busboy. One step higher up the food chain, no pun intended. The cool thing about being a busboy was that you got to pick through the leftovers before the dishwashers got to them.

I don't know if you're aware or not, but there are a lot of drunks working as cooks. Almost every night one of the cooks would be passed out on the kitchen floor. I got promoted to salad chef pretty quickly, not because I was sober, but because I was the last one standing. Eventually I defaulted my way up to fry cook. And finally, of course, I ended up preparing the surf and turf. God help you if you sent something back to the kitchen.

The rest I pretty much learned by hook or by crook. If I found a dish I liked in a restaurant, I would go home and try to figure out how they prepared it, what spices they used. Sometimes you just end up throwing things together in a pot because that's all you've got.

CPSIA information can be obtained at www.ICGtesting.com
Printed in the USA
LVOW091938040413

327687LV00002B/11/A